PRE-READER

Hang On, Monkey!

Susan B. Neuman

NATIONAL GEOGRAPHIC

Washington, D.C.

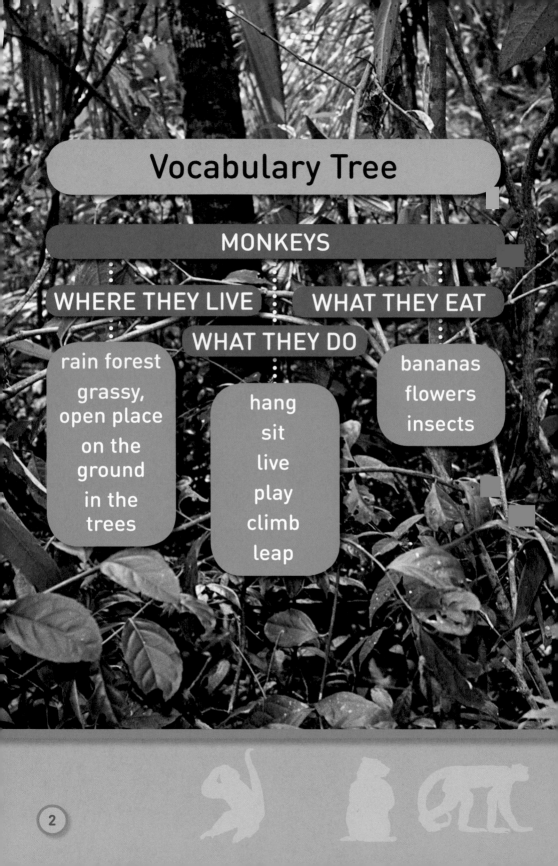

Vocabulary Tree

MONKEYS

WHERE THEY LIVE

WHAT THEY EAT

WHAT THEY DO

WHERE THEY LIVE
rain forest
grassy, open place
on the ground
in the trees

WHAT THEY DO
hang
sit
live
play
climb
leap

WHAT THEY EAT
bananas
flowers
insects

golden lion tamarin

Hang on, monkey!

This monkey hangs on a tree.

northern muriquis

It lives in a rain forest.

vervet monkeys

Monkeys live and play together.

proboscis monkeys

snow monkey

François' leaf monkey

Some live in the trees.

There are small monkeys.

golden lion tamarins

mandrill

There are big monkeys.

Climb, monkey!

red howler monkeys

proboscis monkey

Leap, monkey!

snow monkey

Monkeys like to eat

anything that smells good.

long-tailed macaque

They eat bananas,

Angola colobus

squirrel monkeys

flowers, and even insects.

Monkeys like to hang around.

squirrel monkeys

Hang on, monkey!

Monkey Habitat Map

Monkeys live all over the world. Here's where these monkeys live.

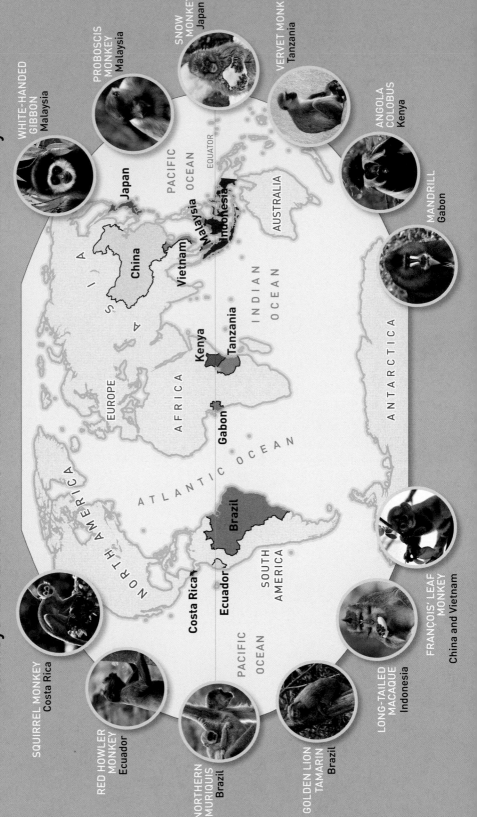

WHITE-HANDED GIBBON
Malaysia

PROBOSCIS MONKEY
Malaysia

SNOW MONKEY
Japan

VERVET MONKEY
Tanzania

ANGOLA COLOBUS
Kenya

MANDRILL
Gabon

FRANÇOIS' LEAF MONKEY
China and Vietnam

LONG-TAILED MACAQUE
Indonesia

GOLDEN LION TAMARIN
Brazil

NORTHERN MURIQUIS
Brazil

RED HOWLER MONKEY
Ecuador

SQUIRREL MONKEY
Costa Rica

PACIFIC OCEAN

EQUATOR

AUSTRALIA

ASIA

Japan

China

Vietnam

Malaysia

Indonesia

INDIAN OCEAN

EUROPE

AFRICA

Kenya

Tanzania

Gabon

ATLANTIC OCEAN

Brazil

Costa Rica

Ecuador

NORTH AMERICA

SOUTH AMERICA

PACIFIC OCEAN

ANTARCTICA

YOUR TURN!

Act like a monkey!

Where do you live?
What do you do?
What do you eat?

Trade paperback ISBN: 978-1-4263-1755-2
Reinforced library edition ISBN: 978-1-4263-1756-9

Book design by David M. Seager

Photo Credits

Cover, Beverly Joubert/National Geographic Creative; 1, Jean-Paul Ferrero/Auscape/Minden Pictures; 2-3, Luciano Candisani/Minden Pictures; 4-5, Luciano Candisani/Minden Pictures; 6-7, Jeff Mauritzen/NGS; 8-9, Barbara Walton/epa/Corbis; 10, Roy Toft/National Geographic Creative; 11, Aflo/naturepl.com; 12, Chris Balcombe/Rex Features; 13, Anup Shah/The Image Bank/Getty Images; 14, Pete Oxford/Minden Pictures; 15, Suzi Eszterhas/Minden Pictures; 16-17, Akira Sato/Nature Production/Minden Pictures; 18, Alain Davreux/Flickr/Getty Images; 18-19, Konrad Wothe/Minden Pictures; 19, Roy Toft/National Geographic Creative; 20-21, Thomas Marent/Minden Pictures; 22 (white-handed gibbon), Jean-Paul Ferrero/Auscape/Minden Pictures; (proboscis monkey), Barbara Walton/epa/Corbis; (snow monkey), Roy Toft/National Geographic Creative; (vervet monkey), Jeff Mauritzen/NGS; (Angola colobus), Konrad Wothe/Minden Pictures; (mandrill), Anup Shah/The Image Bank/Getty Images; (François' leaf monkey), AFLO/naturepl.com; (long-tailed macaque), Alain Davreux/Flickr Select/Getty Images; (golden lion tamarin), Luciano Candisani/Minden Pictures; (northern muriquis), Luciano Candisani/Minden Pictures; (red howler monkey), Pete Oxford/Minden Pictures; (squirrel monkey), Thomas Marent/Minden Pictures; 23, Alain Mafart-Renodier/Biosphoto; 24 (top), Tim Laman/National Geographic Creative; 24 (bottom), Eric Isselée/Shutterstock

National Geographic supports K—12 educators with ELA Common Core Resources.
Visit natgeoed.org/commoncore for more information.

Printed in the United States of America
14/WOR/1